T0277227

Lies, Passions
& Illusions

Lies, Passions
& Illusions

THE DEMOCRATIC IMAGINATION
IN THE TWENTIETH CENTURY

François Furet

Edited with an Introduction by Christophe Prochasson
Translated by Deborah Furet

The University of Chicago Press
Chicago and London

FRANÇOIS FURET (1927–1997) was professor at the École des Hautes Études en Sciences Sociales in Paris and professor in the Committee on Social Thought at the University of Chicago. His many works include *Interpreting the French Revolution*, *The Passing of an Illusion: The Idea of Communism in the Twentieth Century*, and *In the Workshop of History*, the latter two published by the University of Chicago Press.
DEBORAH FURET is François Furet's widow and frequent translator and works at the École des Hautes Études en Sciences Sociales.

Originally published as Inventaires du communisme
© Éditions de l'EHESS, 2012

The University of Chicago Press, Chicago 60637
The University of Chicago Press, Ltd., London
© 2014 by The University of Chicago
All rights reserved. Published 2014.
Printed in the United States of America

23 22 21 20 19 18 17 16 15 14   1 2 3 4 5

ISBN-13: 978-0-226-11449-1 (cloth)
ISBN-13: 978-0-226-15730-6 (e-book)
DOI: 10.7208/CHICAGO/9780226157306.001.0001

Library of Congress Cataloging-in-Publication Data
Furet, François, 1927–1997, author.
    [Inventaires du communisme. English]
    Lies, passions, and illusions : the democratic imagination in the twentieth century / François Furet ; edited with an introduction by Christophe Prochasson ; translated by Deborah Furet.
        pages ; cm
    Includes bibliographical references and index.
    ISBN 978-0-226-11449-1 (hardcover : alk. paper) — ISBN 978-0-226-15730-6 (e-book)   1. Communism—History—20th century.   2. Communism—Soviet Union—History.   I. Prochasson, Christophe, editor, writer of introduction.   II. Furet, Deborah, translator.   III. Title.
HX40.F86413   2014
335.43—dc23

2014002448

♾ This paper meets the requirements of ANSI/NISO z39.48-1992 (Permanence of Paper).

Contents

Cher François Furet,

cette exploration, à travers
des penseurs que nous
estimons, de l'espace
public que vous habitez
en grand historien

Paul R[...]

The book you are about to read is not merely what may be François Furet's last published work. It is also a little adventure in publishing. Among the first volumes of the "Audiographie" series conceived by Philippe Artières and Jean-François Bert for the Éditions de l'EHESS and founded on the notion that spoken texts transcribed may shine light not only on their authors' ideas but also upon the way they think, this book was born of a conversation. Unlike Furet's other works, which were written on yellow legal pads as he worked for long hours alone at his desk, this one emerged from cordial exchanges between two men, each of whom embodied a lifetime of reflection.

Christophe Prochasson, the godfather of the series, who was writing Furet's biography while meticulously overseeing and editing this text, has kindly given me carte blanche to pursue the adventure a little further. His introduction will guide the reader through the way in which the book was pieced together and the additions and changes wrought during that process. What I have done, along with the editors at the University of Chicago Press, was to continue coaxing it from its expository incarnation toward a tighter and more fluent essay. Thus we have eliminated bracketed glosses, typographical distinctions between taped and revised sections, and certain footnotes, including all references to the tape recordings. The original publication, of course, remains available in French.

Sincere and affectionate thanks to Margaret Mahan, who has worked with the Furets since 1987, for her role in the buffing of this jewel-like reflection on the democratic passion.

François Furet and Paul Ricoeur

A DIALOGUE INTERRUPTED

Christophe Prochasson

A former militant of the French Communist Party, which he had joined in 1949 and from which he gradually distanced himself after the repression of the Hungarian uprising in 1956,[1] François Furet had always been animated by a reflection on politics anchored in his own past. He never did stop thinking about the spell of Communism and how, according to him, it blurred our comprehension of things — whether historical as in the case of the French Revolution, strictly political as in the case of the Soviet Union, or having more generally to do with Communism in its historical incarnation. He fought relentlessly against the Communist history of the

French Revolution and, in keeping with this initial battle, enlarged the spectrum of his analyses to include, once the Bicentennial of the Revolution was over and the Berlin Wall had fallen, the history of the "Communist illusion."

He set to work at the very beginning of the 1990s, gathering Communist material, reopening well worked-over dossiers, linking new studies to older surveys and preoccupations. Furet's historiographical turning point became manifest in a long article published in the review *Le Débat*.[2] Then, in October 1990, the historian published a paper entitled "L'énigme de la désagrégation communiste" in the *Notes de la Fondation Saint-Simon*. This was the germ of what, a few years later, would become *The Passing of an Illusion*.

Reprinted by *Le Figaro* in the form of two articles on 21 and 22 November 1990, and by *Le Débat* in its November–December issue, this "Note" would establish François Furet as one of the great analysts of the end of Communism. Charles Ronsac, an editor at the publishers Robert Laffont who also happened to

be François and Deborah Furet's neighbor in Saint
Pierre-Toirac in Southwestern France, encouraged
him to turn the article into a more substantial book.[3]
Thus the author of *Penser la révolution française* shifted
his regard to another century that seemed to resound
with the tragic fulfillment of the promises contained
in the revolutionary message he had studied for so
many years. The "hideous book,"[4] deemed so by the
director Jean-Luc Godard in spite of his admiration
for the historian of the French Revolution, was about
to be born.

This was confirmed by the prepublication in a
new *Note de la Fondation Saint-Simon* of one of the
most incisive chapters, placed at the beginning of the
book and entitled "The Revolutionary Passion." In
January 1995, *Le passé d'une illusion* appeared.[5] It was
a publishing success of the first order: seventy thousand copies were sold within a month and a half. Six
months later, the book was still high on *Le Nouvel Observateur*'s best-seller list. In June 1996, the hundred
thousandth copy was sold, and soon the book would
be translated into eighteen languages.[6]

The critical reception was considerable. The book drew the attention of the popular media, literary programs on television and radio, and the principal publications of the written press, as well as that of politicians and major European intellectuals to whom *Le Débat* would provide a forum in a special issue of the journal.[7] Most of the reactions were in support of the book's theses and, more important, expressed admiration for this work as a tour de force. Indeed, some people were irritated by what they perceived to be a sure triumph, as expressed several times by Jean-François Kahn on television.[8] Even the staunchest adversaries of the book's contents could not deny their intellectual respect for such an imposing work: "The qualities of *Le passé d'une illusion: Essai sur l'idée communiste au XXe siècle* are immediately striking: the sweeping narrative is impressive, the evocation [of events] is powerful and suggestive, the analysis is stimulating and subtle, the style is both dense and incisive,"[9] wrote Denis Berger and Henri Maler, both products of Trotskyism. The only violently negative reactions came from the intellectual Far Left. Others would add their voices, especially in the first decade of the twentieth century, during a critical backlash against the 1980s and 1990s. Furet would be among those accused and judged guilty for finishing off the great ideals that had forged the Left in the century that had just come to an end.[10]

How can we explain this success? There was not much left to reveal about Communism. The macabre bookkeeping that had nourished the great tradition of anti-Communist literature seemed to have passed. Although he was very careful not to hide the sinister character of the Soviet regime while describing its mechanisms of seduction, Furet's contribution was not denunciatory. He too knew, and often affirmed with regret, that the Communist experience of earlier generations did nothing for the generations that would follow and harbor the same illusions. For this indeed was the object of the book: not to compose a historical narrative, but to explain the power of the revolutionary passion incarnated by the Communist idea in the twentieth century. Not to denounce, but to understand. The objectification of the phenomenon and, even more so, the "enigma" of its disappearance were what made this work so effective and so irritating to those who didn't share its conclusions.

Circumstances surely played a role in the favorable reception of a work of this scope, as they had done in the brilliant success of Solzhenitsyn's *The Gulag Archipelago* twenty years earlier. A generation separates these two books, but they belong to the same ideological current. The long process of leaving Communism, which had begun by the mid-1970s and touched not only a few groups of individuals generally belonging to the intelligentsia but whole segments of "left-wingers," came to an end with the end of the century; it was this terminal phase that interested François Furet. His book is an autopsy as well as a death certificate. The agony justifies all his audacity, as when a forensic surgeon allows himself to treat a cadaver ruthlessly. The comparison between Nazism and Communism and, worse still, the perverse dialectic they seemed to share are among Furet's most provocative contentions.

On this point, many reproached Furet for having engaged in a dialogue with the German historian Ernst Nolte, author of a vast, three-volume study of Fascism. Nolte's closeness to the German Right had made him all but a pariah, especially since the *Historikerstreit* of the 1980s, when German historians of National Socialism and Fascism squared off. The comparability of Nazism, Fascism, and Communism was one of Nolte's most controversial themes. Furet wasn't one to be bothered by this sort of taboo, ready as he always was to denounce the intellectual conformism that the Left, in his opinion, was too comfortable with. Perhaps the *Historikerstreit* brought back vivid memories of the tumultuous historiographical and political controversies over his own interpretation of the French Revolution.

He first made known his objections to Nolte's theses in a long footnote in *The Passing of an Illusion*, all the more stunning since the book has very few notes.[11] Even while praising Nolte for having broken with the "anti-Fascist" interpretation of history that prohibited the juxtaposition of the two forms of twentieth-century totalitarianism, he expressed disagreement with Nolte's interpretation of anti-Semitism: according to Furet, the "rational" justification of Nazi anti-Semitism is at once "shocking and false."

The Italian Journal *Liberal* suggested that the two protagonists pursue their exchanges long-distance. From the end of 1995, the two historians began a correspondence that would continue through 1996. The letters were published in France and Italy in *Commentaire* and *Liberal* in the course of 1997. The entire correspondence was published in Italy that same year, the two men having met for the first time a few months earlier in 1996 during a colloquium at the Fondazione Ugo Spirito in Naples.[12] They would meet only once again at a colloquium on liberalism organized in Naples in June 1997, a few weeks before Furet's sudden death on 12 July.

Perhaps Furet regretted this late discussion for having given the impression, most often to his adversaries, that the historian of the French Revolution felt ambivalent or had ultimately converted to a conservative position. In any case, from a reading of the interview that follows, we can glean elements that shed light on his encounter with Nolte, for which Paul Ricoeur, incidentally, did not in the least reproach him. The interview does seem like a last attempt to justify that encounter. Furet was immune to intimidation; nonetheless, while taking responsibility for his choices—the last letter he wrote to Nolte, a few days before his death, praised the "breadth and intelligent generosity" of Nolte's historical analysis of liberalism[13]—he occasionally found that they left a bitter taste.

If the crossing of the paths taken by Nolte and Furet was not a total surprise, the encounter between Furet and the philosopher Paul Ricoeur was a lot more unexpected. Certainly, the two French academics were both affiliated with the University of Chicago, where they had been teaching regularly, Ricoeur since 1970, Furet since 1980. This proximity, however, was without consequence. The two men didn't socialize, although they had met at the university.[14]

Their intellectual and political itineraries could not have been more distinct. No two bodies of work could have been more dissimilar. And although they were both intellectuals with boundless curiosity, one could not have found two men with more divergent sensibilities or centers of interest.

There is evidence of an encounter between Furet and Ricoeur on 4 March 1989, when Furet gave a lecture to the Société française de philosophie on the changing historiography of the French Revolution. In the course of the debate—which, notably, included the participation of Maurice de Gandillac, André Sernin, and Jacques Merleau-Ponty—Ricoeur posed the following questions:

I would like to ask if you apply to the *course* of the Revolution the same sort of thinking you have proposed for its *origins*. You have emphasized the political actors' initiative and even lucidity as to the sense and implications of their actions. Following Michelet, you have also spoken of the "mystery" of the Revolution, attaching to it this great paradox of ours, namely, how you can take autonomous individuals and compose a political body, a body without a head. Is this the key to the chain of events after 1789 or the Terror?

It seems that once the nation had been proclaimed sovereign, the king had become superfluous. But this was the case in September 1789. Why bring him to trial as well? Why condemn him to death? Why execute him? And why the Terror, when the external danger had been removed? So my question is this: was this outcome included in the beginning, which alone would count as an origin? Or did the course of events also come with its own discontinuities and unpredictable choices?[15]

Furet's response was brief and nonetheless contained praise, if a bit conventional, for the philosopher's work: "May I tell you, sir, what a great interest historians take in your books and especially in your thoughts on the discipline they practice."[16] For the rest, Furet responded in a few sentences, with revisions, in the analysis he developed with Denis Richet in their history of the French Revolution.[17] End of conversation.[18]

So a small miracle was needed to bring Furet and Ricoeur together to talk to each other and engage in an examination of the Communist century. It would come from the philosopher François Azouvi, then an editor at Calmann-Lévy, the publishing house

to which, along with Robert Laffont, Furet attributed the success of *The Passing of an Illusion*. Having
published that same year *La critique et la convention*,
a series of interviews with Paul Ricoeur,[19] Azouvi
wished to organize a similar encounter between the
philosopher and the historian. Given the importance
of Furet's book, its exceptional success, its nature—
halfway between history and philosophy—how
could it not hold the attention of a philosopher like
Paul Ricoeur, who never ceased questioning historians about their methods and ways of thinking and
writing? Azouvi had heard Ricoeur express his admiration for *The Passing of an Illusion*, which he had read
with pen in hand.

Still, Furet's big book was not the kind of study
on which Ricoeur would base his representation of
the historian and his work. Conversely, the epistemology of history was a scientific exercise to which
Furet devoted little effort and of which he was rather
skeptical. *The Passing of an Illusion* is still shelved in
a prominent place in Ricoeur's library, and a dozen
pages in that copy are covered with notes in his own

hand; it is difficult to extrapolate from these notes his overall opinion of the book. On these pages, frank enthusiasm encounters doubtful perplexity: "How can one be so peremptory?"; "The historical argument is really good"; "What kind of history?"; "Related to *Penser la Révolution française*"; "Treaty on ideological passions"; "But is the closure total?"; "Brilliant portrait of the bourgeois"; and so on.[20]

The conversation between Furet and Ricoeur took place on 27 May 1996. It was recorded—although the tapes were not preserved—and immediately transcribed. The traces of this first exchange have been preserved in Furet's archives in the Centre d'études sociologiques et politiques Raymond Aron (CESPRA) of the École des hautes études en sciences sociales (EHESS). Unpublishable in its original state, unstructured, full of colloquialisms, the manuscript left much to be desired but, according to Azouvi, its presumed editor, was full of promise. Furet and Ricoeur were thus invited to continue their dialogue as soon as possible. "François Azouvi seems in favor of pursuing and deepening our conversation: at least this will afford me the pleasure of seeing you again soon, this winter."[21] Owing to the busy lives of these two great intellectuals, the dossier remained closed for several months. It was reopened the following spring, when they met again on 19 March 1997.

A few days earlier, on 6 March, Furet had written a long letter to his interlocutor.[22] This letter sought to set out a structure for the verbal exchange and proposed a reorganization of the material. In practical terms, this meant removing all the conversational parts from the transcription of the recording. Vague, spontaneous elements as well as ill-chosen expressions, all of which horrified Furet, had to be replaced by a smooth and well-articulated text with an organization that reflected the movement of thought in progress. It is a very interesting letter, for it plainly reveals the work of transforming an oral text into a written one and brings to light the sort of betrayal or even deceit that the historian and the philosopher had to accept in order to render presentable what Furet considered to be all but obscene babble: "I will shudder when reading these pages (because of all the mistakes in my spoken language)," he wrote to Ricoeur on 22 September.[23] As suggested below, his severity was excessive.

What text did he propose? When writing, Furet applied all the care of an author who had spent years steeped in the novels of Flaubert. One cannot live in daily contact with Chateaubriand and the great authors of the nineteenth century without absorbing certain rules of literary excellence. For all this, Furet was in no way a language aesthete who could be carried away by beautiful sonorities alone or content himself with the quality of his images. His first concern was finding the right word, whose beauty would emerge from its appropriateness. Thus he would organize the first part of the interview around the words "illusion" and "lie":

The two notions are not overlapping because the lie is a deliberate act of trickery and the illusion is an error brought on by the play of passions upon the imagination; Communism was indeed the object of a systematic lie, as testified to, for example, by the trips organized for naive tourists and, more generally, the role attributed to *agit-prop* (militant propaganda) in the movement, but its main force came from elsewhere: its hold over the political imagination of twentieth-century people. That is the origin of its mysterious universality, which the lie alone was incapable of cloaking. This is the aspect I wish to study: the history of a belief. What makes this history so strange is (1) that the belief recognized "real" history as its tribunal and (2) that it nevertheless survived the most spectacular refutations of that so-called "real" history. In short, how can a historian account for a hope grafted onto a tragedy?[24]

The second part would flow easily from these first reflections. Furet thus proposed to Ricoeur that they undertake a comparison between political belief and religious belief. Such an undertaking implied a total change in the order of the conversation, since the initial interview had neglected this dimension, which only emerged from the exchanges in a fairly superficial form. We see here the extent to which Furet perceived oral production as raw material to be transformed into a final product worthy of being presented not to listeners but to readers.

Then came a third phase. Neither interlocutor was chary with analyses: what Furet called the "spell" of October, to which he would devote a long and dense chapter in *The Passing of an Illusion*, was at the center of the conversation: "As to this, it is merely a question of resuming the thread of the discussion, fleshing out certain passages (for example, the relationship between the universal and the national in democratic culture, a question we go over too quickly). These themes constitute the core of our discussion."[25]

It would be easy to go from an examination of the "illusion" strictly speaking to "an analysis of the concept of totalitarianism, its reach and its limits."[26] This concept is not a familiar one to Furet, who rarely used it and who often, while deploring the abuses to which it led, pointed out the political agenda that sometimes motivated condemnations of its employment. In this section he would bring up, not unexpectedly, many related questions such as the possibility of comparing the Nazi and Soviet regimes as well as the relations between these regimes and democratic modernity. Furet also foretold the discussion of Claude Lefort's theses on totalitarian power, conceived as the place of the "reincorporation of democratic individuals within a collective being by reducing the many to One, and in a sort of archaic return to the idea of a political body."[27]

The published interview could end, wrote Furet, with the future of post-Communist democracy "using indispensable prudence." This concern, at the heart of Furet's "melancholy" at the end of his life, seems to have come up often in his exchanges with Ricoeur. In a filmed interview produced in 1997, a few weeks after Furet's death, the philosopher returned to the comparison of the two totalitarianisms, a concept about which he had "reservations." For Ricoeur, the two utopias were "not comparable" although there were many similarities in the means they employed. And the philosopher resumed the dialogue with the recently deceased historian by saying the latter had been correct in thinking that, by killing off the great utopia that had structured Western consciences, the end of Enlightenment optimism had left humankind without a future. Henceforth, what would become of the revolutionary passions engendered by democracy, which was always too procedural to satisfy those passions? That question, Ricoeur affirmed, haunted the correspondence — sadly incomplete — exchanged by these two men during the months in which they prepared the book of interviews that would never see the day.[28]

The text that follows is of a hybrid nature, the fruit of an encounter between three authors of obviously very distinct statuses. The principal author — the only one with the moral right of signature — is incontestably François Furet. The text is one of the last on which he worked. His working archives contain a version dated June 1997, which incorporates the handwritten corrections that figure on an earlier version corresponding to the exact transcription of the exchanges. This 1997 version provides the basis for the text published here.

The other authors are invisible but not imperceptible. Ricoeur's part has been deleted with the agreement of the directors of the Fonds Ricoeur, for the following reason. Furet's death interrupted a work in progress which, insofar as his part was concerned, was further developed and in fact finished. Ricoeur had not yet had the chance to work on the project when he learned that Furet had died. His own analyses, directly transcribed from the recording, were much less developed than those of Furet, who had added many developments to the discussion, specifying, qualifying, or correcting his part of the interview, sometimes eliminating whole sentences or even paragraphs. Ricoeur never completed his revisions, since he felt that the dialogue had become impossible after Furet's death. He probably felt uncomfortable about revising a text in the absence of one of the authors, since Furet had submitted his own modifications to him.

Like Jeffrey Barash, a philosopher who had worked closely with Ricoeur since the 1970s (the period during which he was also teaching at the University of Chicago) and whom François Azouvi had asked to conduct the debates (he sometimes spoke at length during the discussion), Ricoeur has become an invisible interlocutor. As we shall see, his absence is not total. The historian reacts to the philosopher's remarks, to his analysis, to his replies, and sometimes to his objections. A reader who listens closely can sometimes make out the philosopher's voice or at least get an idea of it and can thus imagine the sound, or more precisely the tone, of the interview.

In closing, I would like to say a few words about the most passive and least creative of the authors, that is, the editor of the text. Scientific rigor or, more simply, intellectual honesty should keep us from hiding the role of this third author, although he may be one from the minor leagues. Nonetheless, he is responsible for the final form of the text and in some ways its conception; this responsibility merits some explanation so as to inform the reader and to remain loyal to the memory of François Furet.

The guiding principle was as simple as can be: to respect the integrity of the words set down by Furet in his 1997 draft. Since Furet was so careful about the literary form of his writings, the order of the text, which follows the course of the conversation, has been respected, with only two exceptions. These two slight shifts, which reinforce the general coherence of Furet's remarks, are signaled in the French edition of this book (but not in this translation) by notes in which I indicate the cassettes' number and sides. I also thought it useful to introduce headings corresponding to the themes announced by Furet in his long letter of 6 March 1997 to Ricoeur. Last, occasional colloquialisms that evoke the conversational origins of the published text have been left largely intact, though respecting Furet's aversion to colloquialisms in his own writing, we have occasionally removed them.

In Furet's case, it is not a given that the oral always appears in a more relaxed form than the written, even if there are obvious differences between certain recorded passages and the text rewritten by Furet. Sometimes, he erased a passage he found poorly formulated. One example is enough to show how he transformed the oral into the written. In the first pages of the first version of the interview, Furet questioned the Soviet Union's incarnation of the Communist idea in these terms:

Because one can easily say—and that is in fact what people say to me—that the history of the Soviet Union has nothing to do with the Communist idea. And, consequently, the Communist idea is still intact. I totally agree. In politics, this is a completely defensible point of view. But a historian cannot defend this, since I can show that fifty years ago, the Communist idea was the Soviet Union. Thirty years ago, the Communist idea was the Soviet Union. So today we can dress up history by forgetting the experience of the Soviet Union, or by saying that it had nothing to do with Communism, but that would not be historically defensible. It is politically justifiable.[29]

Furet threw out this passage and substituted the following paragraph:

The Communist idea, as an abstract idea, did not die with the disappearance of the Soviet Union. To the extent that it was born of the frustrations inseparable from capitalist society, and from the hatred of a world dominated by money, it is independent of its "realization"; all it needs is the abstract hope of a postcapitalist universe. Nonetheless, from that time on, it also had a history whose losses were impossible to write off, as has been attempted here and there on the Left. But one could certainly neutralize this history by saying that the Soviet Union never had anything to do with socialism or Communism; or, turning to the Trotskyist version, by saying that everything was fine until 1924 and then everything went badly. But who could believe these denials? The truth of the century, a truth witnessed by so many, not all of whom were amnesiacs, is that the Soviet Union, throughout its history, managed to incarnate the Communist hope, in the minds of millions and millions of our contemporaries, during every period of the regime's existence. It is this mystery of incarnation, the universalistic mystery of such a special and tragic history, that I am trying to understand.[30]

The text we shall now discover has but a distant relationship to the oral version. What interest, then, does it hold when compared to other texts that Furet published in a variety of different periodicals, conceived and written as publishable texts and dealing with the same themes, in the wake of the appearance of *The Passing of an Illusion*? The answer is not obvious, since Furet constantly issued written or oral commentaries to explain the themes of his work, to respond to hasty or malicious interpretations, to better express certain propositions, or to respond to criticisms. The nature of Furet's style was to return again and again to the same propositions and expressions, as if doing so allowed them to be both polished and reinforced. This practice seemed quite deliberate and led him to publish the same texts in a variety of places in order to increase their visibility. The same strategy can be discerned in his recourse to certain expressions repeated word for word, circulating seamlessly, from oral to written, from interviews to discussions, from lectures to conference proceedings, but also in articles in learned journals and the press, in scientific works and articles in *Le Nouvel Observateur*. Furet's style was of a piece. No matter what he thought, his oral language was very controlled and closely related to his writing style. He made no stylistic concessions to the "general public" and used the same style in his popular and his learned publications. Since Furet rejected any esoteric forms or jargon, his writing is completely without obscurity.

The particular interest of the text presented here is that it gathers together Furet's final considerations on *The Passing of an Illusion*, a book that would be his last and that brought him international fame. These considerations could thus be construed as an intellectual testament. A political testament as well, for they resume the author's latest fears about the future of democracy. There are no really new ideas if we consider the numerous other works on the subject, but we can spot a few ultimate adjustments, which lend these reflections a touching dimension. These reflections are, moreover, exempt from the expressions Furet was regularly employing during months in which *The Passing of an Illusion* was the object of constant commentary. A slight distancing is noticeable, opening the door to self-criticism and the toning down of certain chapters central to the book. We saw this apropos of Nolte. We will see it in the passages on totalitarianism: Furet always kept a critical distance from this concept, aware as he was of the abuses and laziness it brought out in certain authors. He returns to the concept one last time with determination.

So the reader has been advised. As with any edited text, the following pages do not come directly from the past. Like a meteorite entering the atmosphere, transformed by a long and perilous course, this discourse has undergone important modifications passing from the oral universe to the hard reality of writing. From one point of view, the transformation is painful because it implies a loss. Furet's phrasing, his breathing still burdened by a long-vanquished tuberculosis, lent his speech a special tone. On the other hand, the critical obligations required by the metamorphosis from oral to written elucidate the subject in a way often lacking in more spontaneous speech. Furthermore, as an editor I have thrown in my own grain of salt. By making this clear, I hope to be considered less a troublemaker than a discreet *metteur en texte*.

Ideas and Emotions

For the title of my 1995 book, I chose not the "end of the illusion," or the "history of the illusion," but the "passing of an illusion," with an indefinite article, *an* illusion, so as to emphasize that what came to an end before our eyes, and to our surprise, was the illusion of a postcapitalist, postbourgeois society in the forms it had assumed in the twentieth century—that is, in the form of Communist or Soviet regimes we had known. The first chapter of *The Passing of an Illusion* states precisely that to my mind it was not really the end of all the illusions of democratic man; to the contrary, I think modern democracy contains a constitutive illusion born of the demand for autonomy and equality that we have lived with for several centuries. It took on a particular historical form in the twentieth century, and owed much of its strength to the fact that it had ceased to be a project and was now a regime that actually existed. In order to understand October 1917 and the event's extraordinary power of resonance in spite of its improbability—and by improbability I mean the fact that it had happened in that particular place—we must see this event as being part of an expectation. An expectation more than a hundred years old—it could be dated from the French Revolution—the expectation that the ideas of modern democracy would be realized: all people shall and should be equal. Indeed, Marx, in his early works, clearly understood this when he spoke of the "illusion *of* politics" and of the French Revolution as the manifestation of the illusion of politics: people are not equal, citizens are equal in an illusory way. October 1917 filled the gaping hole between person and citizen.[1]

In the nineteenth century, the socialist or Communist idea did not exist anywhere in the sense that it was not in power anywhere. So it was worked with, nurtured, kept alive in every way possible, and everyone imagined it according to his or her own inclinations. Karl Marx and Ferdinand Lasalle, Jules Guesde and Jean Jaurès, Louis Blanc and Proudhon all dreamed of a postcapitalist society, each in his own way.[2] Not until the twentieth century, however, was that plurality narrowed down to a single form of postcapitalist society. And the surprising thing is that when this idea became incarnated in historical reality, instead of becoming weaker it grew stronger, no matter how much it was belied by the course of its regime. That is the illusion we are talking about.

Must there be a lie for there to be an illusion? Not necessarily. One can conceive of a situation in which the need to believe is completely independent of both the object of belief and the affirmations of its reality: psychology offers us examples. An illusion comes from an unfounded belief engendered by the play of passions on the imagination. An old man may believe he is "acting young" simply because this feeling protects him from his proximity to death, while those around him do nothing to maintain the illusion. A lie, to the contrary, is a deliberate act of deceit, by which the liar tries to mislead a third party; the error ceases when the person who benefits from spreading the falsehood is unmasked. Communism was certainly the object of a systematic lie, as testified to, for example, by the trips organized for naïve tourists and, more generally, by the extreme attention the Soviet regime and the Communist parties paid to propaganda and brain washing. But this vast collective lie, the object of such deliberate care, was unique for existing within a shared illusion: the liar, in this case, far from feeling that he is tricking the person who is listening to him, is only trying to persuade him of something he believes to be true. If he "arranges" reality, if he never stops thinking of the effect he is having, it is in order not to deceive but to convince: he exaggerates, or even makes things up, which is different from lying. If it is true that lying requires a division within the self between what one thinks and what one says, militant Communists never lie; they are fully at one with what they say.

Moreover, they never place themselves outside the illusion they are committed to propagate. So much so that even when they are victims of the system in which they have faith, even when plunged into the horror of the Gulag, they continue to proclaim their loyalty to Communism. What could better illustrate the persistence of their illusion and the intransigence of their political faith in the face of facts?

Communism's power came not from its material or military strengths — although they were important contributing factors — but from its hold over the political imagination of twentieth-century men and women. It is this hold and its various elements that I attempted to analyze in my book. This is the "illusion" I sought to inventory. I wanted to write the history of a belief that was all the more extraordinary for presenting a priori two contradictory characteristics: on the one hand, this belief, completely modern, was no longer transcendent or religious and could be judged only by the course of "real" history; on the other hand, it survived the most spectacular denials of so-called "real" history and came to an end only with the historical object it served for three-quarters of a century—the Soviet Union itself. The question posed by *The Passing of an Illusion* could be summarized as follows: how can a historian account for a hope grafted onto a tragedy when tragedy was its only reference?

I think the Soviet leaders' program was to liquidate capitalism and build a society where the individual was master of the forces of production, where the society would become an association of individuals working together to domesticate nature: this powerful image of the Soviet Union was current in the West in the early 1930s. What evidence is there that the Soviet leaders did not believe in this image and hold it for true? My opinion is that they too lived in the illusion. As to the cynicism of the Soviet leaders and the Communist leaders, and when their behavior became cynical, these are questions I leave open. It is a very difficult issue to understand, for until the end of the regime, as far as we can tell from the archives, they all spoke as though they believed in the Communist ideology; at no time did a Communist leader, including Mikhail Gorbachev, say he was lying. Was this in order to manipulate the masses?

The history I sought to write is that of the political imagination of democratic citizens of the twentieth century, the intellectual and emotional forces through which individuals make politics. People don't engage in politics for "rational" reasons; they engage in politics because they are emotionally or intellectually drawn to a certain number of ideas, especially on the Left, where the ideas are stronger than those on the Right; what I have tried to do in a general way was to write a history of these ideas and emotions. I am a specialist in the French Revolution and of revolutions in general, periods when emotional, affective, and ideological investment in action is at its height. These are the most difficult periods to interpret. Given the extraordinary force of the revolutionary idea, these are moments of the most intense mediation between intentions and action. I wanted to see how something I studied in the French Revolution—since I cast the Terror largely as a product of revolutionary ideology—was manifested in the twentieth century. Two surprises: first, that the wealth of revolutionary emotions and ideas was invested in a tyrannical regime, easily identified as such; and, second, that this regime, the object of such a powerful psychological investment, turned out to be extraordinarily fragile and would die very rapidly and of itself, unlike all other regimes and empires that we know of.

The End of a World?

The death of the Soviet Union was the opposite of what happened with the Turkish Empire, which clearly was moribund for several centuries and took a long time to die. The Napoleonic Empire, despite its great power, was defeated militarily. The Soviet Empire was not defeated militarily, yet it disappeared as suddenly as the Napoleonic, while suffering, like nineteenth-century Turkey, from a deficit of "civilization." So the characteristics of the way it ended emphasized the extent to which socialism's superiority in principle over capitalism was unfounded. When opened just a crack to liberty, "real" socialism collapsed like a house of cards, incapable of competing with capitalist civilization. Just as Fascism was defeated by brute force along the lines of its own defiance, Soviet Communism perished through its incapacity to fulfill its ambitions for a better society. But the rapidity of its disappearance, so surprising because of its internal nature, underlined the inanity of the Communist pretension and the belief that Communism could incarnate a more civilized future for humanity.

No one is trying to see exactly what ended. Yet it's easy to grasp: 1991 signaled the end of the historically determined form assumed by the Communist illusion in world public opinion. And that illusion lasted as long as the Soviet Union, until and including its last period, the Gorbachev era. For the history of the USSR demonstrably went through several phases, from Lenin to Gorbachev, by way of Stalin and Leonid Brezhnev. But each of them shared the ambition to realize the original promise, a socialist society delivered from the curses of capitalism. Stalin claimed to be perpetuating Lenin; Brezhnev did as best he could to integrate Nikita Khrushchev's critique of Stalin into the legacy; Gorbachev took the (deadly) risk of political pluralism, but without abandoning the dogma of the superiority of socialism over capitalism. In a more general way, the idea of "socialism with a human face," which appeared in 1968 during the Prague "Spring" and was meant to offset part of the Stalinist heritage, was merely a fleeting adjustment to the original image. The adjustment had no effect on the system itself, which remained incompatible with freedom, as its end would show, but was useful nonetheless as an ideological recharge, as attested to by the influence of this "revisionist" Communism in the West. It also explains why Gorbachev failed to put an end to the Communist idea in both its hard and "soft" versions.

The Communist idea, as an abstract idea, did not die with the disappearance of the Soviet Union. To the extent that it was born of the frustrations inseparable from capitalist society, and from the hatred of a world dominated by money, it is independent of its "realization"; all it needs is the abstract hope of a postcapitalist universe. Nonetheless, from that time on, it also had a history whose losses were impossible to write off, as has been attempted here and there on the Left. But one could certainly neutralize this history by saying that the Soviet Union never had anything to do with socialism or Communism; or, turning to the Trotskyist version, by saying that everything was fine until 1924 and then everything went badly. But who could believe these denials? The truth of the century, a truth witnessed by so many, not all of whom were amnesiacs, is that the Soviet Union, throughout its history, managed to incarnate the Communist hope, in the minds of millions and millions of our contemporaries, during every period of the regime's existence. It is this mystery of incarnation, the universalistic mystery of such a special and tragic history, that I am trying to understand.

On the Nation

The French Revolution sought to found the modern social contract exclusively upon history, its own history. Michelet and Quinet were well aware of it. Michelet said that the French Revolution was a religion. But that's precisely what it was not: it could never have been a religion, in spite of its political actors' pathetic attempts. The great misfortune of the French Revolution as compared to the English or American revolutions was that the time for religions had passed and that democracy was born in France in an era when religion could no longer be called upon in imagining the political city. Hence, even the conflict with the Catholic Church was not lived out in its philosophical profundity. This is the gist of Quinet's critique. Under Napoleon, the French Revolution would end up instrumentalizing the church, letting it fall victim to modern democracy—something the French in particular, though not they alone, have witnessed for two centuries. I once felt that the Communist mystique, which I experienced personally at one point in my life, was the quintessence of that history. It was, par excellence, a total psychological investment in history in order to bring about the salvation of humanity as well as individual salvation. The circumstantial element here, into which I introduce the notions of mystery and enigma, is that things went miraculously badly, to use Joseph de Maistre's characterization of the French Revolution.[1] First there was the World War of 1914–18; then that amazing event in Russia—it could have happened elsewhere: it was the worst point of departure for the Communist revolution.

The international socialist movement's claim at the turn of the nineteenth century, to go beyond the horizon of nations and thus form an avant-garde that would carry the interests of all humanity, was shown, when tested by events, to be unrealistic. Moreover, not just in 1914 but in the course of the twentieth century and until recently, national or nationalist passion proved far more motivating than internationalist or cosmopolitan sentiments. For all that, it is clear today, at least in Western Europe (a West including Germany), that many disasters brought on by the spirit of nationalist overbidding have actually strengthened the idea of humanity. That, of course, is where democracy leads its citizens, since its ambition is the emancipation of universal man and woman, its ultimate goal the peaceful organization of all of humanity. But its movement is impeded by an earlier idea of community, formed before it, by and around the European monarchies: the nation was its first crucible, so much so that in the twentieth century it almost became its tomb.

This was the drama that came to a head in the summer of 1914. In the name of the nation, the popular masses of Europe entered into modern political civilization pitted against one another. What should have been accomplished, according to the prophets of democracy, through schooling and through an apprenticeship in the universal was wrought by war like an exaltation of the particular. Even intellectuals, in an unprecedented manner, joined in the general chauvinism. Of the two images of community—humanity and the nation—that peopled the democratic imagination, the second erased the first. But not forever, since the interminable suffering to which they were subjected by war exhausted the people's patience, and the sense of the universal was revived by a desire for peace, which would be the mainspring of the Russian Revolution. But the dice of history thrown in August 1914 continued to roll, and the massacre could only be stopped by the total victory of one camp and the capitulation of the other: an extreme solution that carried public opinion toward nationalist extremism. So Europe's first democratic and industrial war heated up the ideas and emotions that led, on one hand, to Communism, the new version of the universal, and, on the other, to Fascism, the hysterical form of nationalist passion. The political chemistry that had nourished the French revolutionary adventure — an unstable mixture of the universal and the national — at the dawn of democracy had reconstituted its two poles little more than a century later, this time, like sparks across Europe, with Russia the country of internationalism and Germany the country of nationalism.

Before Hitler, at the turn of the nineteenth and twentieth centuries, there was a great deal of connivance and demagoguery on the part of the ruling classes, who used this lever for their own ends to instrumentalize the popular masses' entry into politics. There was a whole bunch of French, German, Russian, and Austrian nationalists in the late nineteenth and early twentieth century; all historians are aware that by the end of the nineteenth century a new political landscape had emerged, which could be called democratic insofar as the masses were involved. The masses were the great dread of nineteenth-century European bourgeoisies: how could they be handled? This is clear from the bourgeoisies' scared reaction to universal suffrage when, after all, there is nothing terribly scary about it. But the only way for the ruling classes to tame the masses was through upping nationalism, and that is one of the fundamental reasons for World War I. In the event, one can hardly feel indulgence for the ruling classes.

At the turn of the nineteenth century and on into the twentieth, something happened that is almost incomprehensible today: a surrender to nationalist craziness, to the arrogance of national superiority. Intellectuals were major stakeholders in this surrender. Zeev Sternhell, in spite of the problems posed by his approach, wrote some interesting things about what was going on at the time;[2] all the nations in Europe were experiencing a kind of nationalist drift.

Enthusiasm for war or, at least, public opinion's prior consent to the war is probably the basic reason for the outbreak of the conflict. It was by relying on these prowar sentiments in each of their countries that the leaders of the great powers could behave so chauvinistically and, in the end, irresponsibly in the summer of 1914. It was a state of mind that set the scene; the German-Slavic rivalry in the Balkans and the other Franco-German or Anglo-German antagonisms merely inflamed it. This state of mind has disappeared so completely that it has become all but unintelligible, as is the case with the peoples' capacity, once the war broke out, to bear the suffering it imposed and to pay the price with their blood. It's true that these were still largely agricultural peoples, less accustomed than we are to the amenities of life; for a historian, however, their capacity to bear so much misfortune for such a long time remains very surprising.

After the Napoleonic wars, the Treaty of Vienna was put together in the framework of European civilization by means of a concurrence among the European monarchies, aristocracies, and ruling classes. There was no rivalry that couldn't be organized in the form of a balance of powers. At the time of which I am now speaking, things were very different: European politics had acquired a new, totally different dimension. Politics had become "democratic" in the Tocquevillian sense of the word; that is, it was henceforth the business of the masses, subject to demagoguery, especially of the nationalist sort. Who could have explained to a French peasant, bourgeois, or worker in 1916 that there had to be a compromise on Alsace-Lorraine? The idea was preposterous. Moreover, Clemenceau used this impasse to establish his authority.

With respect to the idea of nation, I am struck by the twentieth century's constant replay of the drama of 1914. Fascism, of course, was a pathological exaltation of national sentiment. But Communism itself finally went the way of democratic universalism under the French Revolution. It became national. Stalin represents the transformation of Bolshevik universalism into Russian nationalism while still wearing the mask of Bolshevik universalism. In the end, we watched Europe die of its own most brilliant invention: the nation. This is one way of looking at the twentieth century. What Europe brought to the history of the world, as compared to Greek or Roman antiquity, was the nation, which is the historical form of modern civilization. And it all but killed us.

For my part, I am a European because it is the least bad way of being true to the national idea in a very depressed landscape, where Europe is no longer what it was, where it needs to gather its forces, which means its nations, in the face of the storms and the state of the world. But we will pay very dearly, in all sorts of ways, for the incapacity of European bourgeois societies to deal with the phenomenon of nationalism in the twentieth century.

The Socialist Movement, the Nation, and the War

I believe the only way to interpret historically the rise of the socialist movement in France, Germany, and England at the end of the nineteenth century is that it was a means of incorporating the workers, of ending the workers' exile. The nineteenth century was hard on the workers. In France, their exile came to an end only in 1936. In Germany it ended sooner, with Bismarck's State Socialism, one of the great triumphs of social democracy and the German workers' movement. But I don't think the German workers' movement or the German Socialist Party ever had a realistic vision of a socialist regime in Germany. The same goes for France: take, for example, Jaurès, a man for whom I have a profound affection. He was great insofar as he dreamed, in essence, of bringing the workers' movement back into the Republic, of creating something that would become a progressive Left, which he did, in fact, after the Dreyfus Affair. When he spoke of the future of socialism, he left the realm of politics.

The sense of universality is inseparable from democratic consciousness. The socialist idea, in all its forms, seeks to realize its goal historically by emancipating humanity from capitalist alienation. But it collides with the problem of nation, an inheritance from the distant past. The early nineteenth-century socialists underestimated the power of national passions, which divide humanity rather than uniting it.

Even Marx constantly thought of politics in terms of nations. During the Franco-Prussian war of 1870 he sided with Prussia, for he thought the war would bring about German unity and thus further a necessary process. For similar reasons, Marx approved of the British colonization of India and the French colonization of Algeria: he thought they represented a step forward in the universalization of the world. When he spoke of politics, he had a pretty realistic vision of the nation as the central instrument of historical dynamism. And this, it seems to me, though it bears a closer look, was all but lost in the discussions during the Second International.

To my knowledge, European socialist leaders never went very far in this projected union of all workers. No commission was ever set up in an attempt to harmonize their foreign policies, something we now consider a prerequisite of internationalism. And in July 1914, at the last meetings attended by Jaurès, in Brussels, just before he was assassinated, no analysis was going on. There were rhetorical nods to strikes, to the possibility of striking, and so forth. But there was no real analysis of the international situation. The surprising thing about 1914 was that everyone succumbed to fatalism. Never before had there been such a strong sense of human alienation.

The militants of the Second International were faced with very powerful movements of public opinion, and in opposing the war they exposed themselves to accusations of treason. Such was the situation at the end of July and the beginning of August 1914.

I believe Jaurès, without jingoistic enthusiasm, would have been in favor of the Union sacrée and would probably have been an early partisan of a compromise peace, as it might have been imagined in 1915 and 1916. But in 1914, I doubt that it would have been possible for him to spread any other message than that of a "sacred union."

This was all the more true in the French case since France was invaded in the first month of the war and the national collectivity was threatened. More generally, the war gave rise in many quarters to unprecedentedly chauvinistic reactions. Take intellectuals, for example: for the first time in history, Kant was viewed with suspicion in France for being a German philosopher, and Voltaire in Berlin for being a French writer. With the outbreak of the war in 1914, the ravages wrought on people's minds by nationalistic indoctrination could be measured—an indoctrination for which the European political ruling classes were largely responsible, each in its own national context.

Curiously, as I tried to show in *The Passing of an Illusion*, though perhaps not insistently enough, traces of the old aristocratic and martial values still lingered in bourgeois societies; these were values that Adam Smith, Benjamin Constant, and Auguste Comte considered to have been surpassed by the evolution of history.[1] When the masses went to war, they were caught up in the bourgeois world's most elementary passion for belonging, that is, national belonging. In contrast, among the elites—for example, the generation that graduated from the École normale supérieure just prior to 1914—we can see the survival or revival of military and aristocratic values, of self-sacrifice, which were also very powerful in Germany.

There is some truth in Arno Mayer's theory that the nineteenth century can be seen as a predominantly aristocratic period;[2] a time when the European ruling classes were often socially bourgeois while remaining steeped in the old world and the old civilization, in the values of sacrifice and of military and aristocratic heroism. It was true even of the French Republic in that century, to say nothing of Germany. And these values counted for a lot; they appear constantly in texts written on the eve of World War I.

Something about Europe in the late nineteenth century and the first half of the twentieth that seems never to have been well explained is the fact that modern democracy was so passionately nationalistic. From today's standpoint, this is hard to understand. For my part, I experienced the period when the French, just before World War II, were still talking about World War I at every meal. Every family had its dead.

My father was a pacifist. Two of his brothers had died in the war, one at Verdun: my grandmother never stopped referring to them. The disappearance of patriotic values since the end of World War II astounds me by its abruptness. Fascism, of course, had a lot to do with it, by liquidating militarism and war. The two world wars discredited war by taking it to the very extremes of horror and absurdity. In doing so, sadly, they dishonored Europe.

To what extent had the great upheaval of 1914 been prepared for? To what extent had it been written into the history of the Second International? Without knowing for sure, I believe that the Second International brought together very different parties, which were incapable of acting in unison and were very largely middle class. Here I think that Lenin was not all wrong and that the pre–World War I socialist parties, in their respective countries, were well integrated into national life.

Universalism never provides a framework for action. We see this very clearly today with respect to humanitarianism and human rights. Less than ever do these ideas provide a framework for politics; inevitably they bring to mind the words of Pascal: "He who would act the angel, acts the beast." In reality, political action in the nineteenth and twentieth centuries has occurred through the interests and passions of classes and nations. I would say that this was already true during the French Revolution. All the French Revolutionaries spoke of universality. All of them. And they conquered Europe in the name of a "great nation."

The sense and even the passion for universalism constitute the common ground shared by liberalism and democracy, where people are defined less by their particular civic activity than by their economic activity and the enjoyment of their natural rights— two characteristics that define people essentially as members of humanity. They are people of commerce and of the contract projected by the Enlightenment; in this respect, democracy is merely a consequence of liberal principles, which explains the futility of nineteenth-century attempts to hamper its development. But it also explains why democratic universality, which privileges economics, the relationship of humankind to the transformation of nature, suffers from a political deficit and has such a hard time establishing the rule of law and government: modern individuals are free and equal, but their primary preoccupation is their own enrichment and their private happiness. This is particularly noticeable today, at a time when the national bond is loosening in Western European countries: the call to universal rights isn't leading to any political initiative, as shown by the question of immigration.

The Past and the Future of the Revolution

Russian society was shattered between 1917 and 1921; it wasn't Stalin who invented the Terror and the camps. It was during the Tenth Congress, in 1921, that fractions within the Party were banned. We know that Lenin died almost in despair. We see this in his writings, his last articles, his thoughts in 1922, during his remissions from illness: he viewed the situation with great sadness, and there is certainly a difference between Lenin and Stalin. But one cannot conceive of Stalin if there hadn't been a Lenin beforehand.

✦

There is no agreement on the meaning of the word "lie." When speaking of the Soviets' lies, I am not talking about any active lie on the part of Lenin or Trotsky. I'm talking about an objective lie. The lie about the Soviets and the workers' power is the false idea that the Soviets were ever a workers' power or even a democratic one. The lie refers to officially ratified contradictions between words and deeds.

Jacobinism was an ultrarevolutionary experience that preceded the Soviets, but the Soviets installed themselves into it as if it were an earlier form of their own revolution. One of the spells of Bolshevism was that the revolution, which was radically new because it liquidated the bourgeoisie, had precedents in the history of revolutionary voluntarism. So the Bolsheviks played both sides: they laid claim to a tradition while being radically new. And that tradition could only have been Jacobinism, because Jacobinism was where they found dictatorship, the Terror, voluntarism, the exaltation of the new man, and so on. The fascinating thing is that revolution, since the French Revolution, has also become a political tradition, serving as a precedent for October 1917.

I think October and Lenin will make a comeback. Stalin will be liquidated, abandoned. But I think Lenin can still look to a bright future. Especially by way of the Trotskyites, who will—finally—benefit from their status as victims of Stalin. Terrorists victimized by the Terror, their persecution will blot out their role as persecutors. A bit like Danton during the French Revolution. We now see them being reborn: they are in great shape at the moment since they have finally gotten rid of the Stalinists and are renovating the myth. October will always keep something of its original spell, I believe, and remain a founding moment, a dream, an instant torn from history.

Don't forget that behind all this lies the constructivist idea. Society as permanent invention. What is extraordinary, is that this idea should have taken root in Russia, for it was the least appropriate country to incarnate it. I think it has something to do with Russia's foreignness. For centuries, the West had lived with the idea that Russia was a mysterious country from which anything might emerge. You find this perception at the dawn of the modern era. Mystery played no small role in the birth of Soviet mythology. The whole business was so far away, so bizarre. In the West, there was a kind of eschatological vision of Russia, a vision older than Communism.

Even more remarkably, it was in the twentieth century that so many people, because of the Communist idea, imagined that Russia could be not just another European country but the avant-garde of European civilization. Even today, when Russia has ripped off its Communist mask, Europeans don't know what to make of it. Both by habit and by contrast they consider it "liberal" since it is no longer Communist. This is obviously absurd. What we are rediscovering so painfully is how foreign Russia is to Europe.

At the Sorbonne, for seventy years students were taught that the French Revolution was the antechamber for the Russian Revolution.[1] It is amazing that generations of very knowledgeable academics—for Georges Lefebvre was an extraordinary scholar of the French Revolution[2]—could have compared these events, which were hardly comparable: the French Revolution founded a society, enriched the peasantry and the bourgeoisie, and immediately found a remarkably solid social base in the nation; the Russian Revolution crushed the whole society, destroyed the peasantry, and installed a single party. There is nothing comparable about the two revolutions except for the Jacobins.

In this connection, let us compare English and French history. The English had a revolution in the seventeenth century, executed their king, had a brief republican period followed by the restoration of a legitimate dynasty, which was soon interrupted, in 1688, by the call for a new royal family. A sequence of events that can be compared, at least partially, to that of the French Revolution—and heaven knows it has been done, from the 9 Thermidor until today. Nonetheless, the English historiographical tradition, apart from the Marxists, tends to erase the English revolution instead of celebrating it. Whether Tory or Liberal, what historians celebrate is 1688, the end of the revolution, which would become the Glorious Revolution to distinguish it from the one that had preceded it, baptized the Great Rebellion. French historians, on the other hand, have for the past two centuries continuously promoted the French Revolution to the status of a founding event. Even when cursing it, they only emphasize its exceptional character. And no French person on the Right or the Left can remain unmoved by the extraordinary national adventure of that period, constantly heroized in French literature. Why such a contrast?

Several elements must be taken into account. The English revolution of the seventeenth century was steeped in religion. It was animated, down to its most egalitarian characteristics, by militants permeated with biblical culture. Unlike the French in 1789, the English revolutionaries weren't trying to produce a tabula rasa in the face of tradition but, on the contrary, were seeking a return to the golden age of the holy scriptures. Within the span of English history the revolution took its bearings from a period prior to the Norman invasion and thus, unlike 1789 in France, lacked the preeminent dignity of an origin. On the one hand, the English were not deprived of their history prior to Oliver Cromwell; on the other, they reaffirmed and renewed their religious foundation in the form of state Protestantism. In 1688, moreover, their revolution would come to a happy end, erasing the violence and the civil war that marked the period; even the memory of the 1649 regicide would be erased by the reunion of the nation with its new monarchy. By means of its revolution, England managed to consolidate its tradition rather than condemning it.

In French history, the revolutionary idea is inseparable from the democratic idea. There is no way to pry them apart. The democratic idea, the constructivist idea, the idea of human self-creation: it's all inscribed in the idea of the revolution. The reason we are so unhappy today is that we no longer have a revolutionary idea. It is as if our political civilization had been truncated. The socialists were cast as inferior to the Communists throughout the twentieth century because they were incapable of incarnating a revolution. When I was an adolescent, at the end of World War II, the idea that one could be a reformist was incomprehensible to me because it seemed so inadequate in proportion to the events we were experiencing—such a narrow, mediocre, and unattractive idea. When the Red Army took over Berlin and crushed Nazism, it gave the Bolshevik revolutionary idea an incomparable and truly universal radiance, an imaginary power that must be restored, and it's up to historians to do so, since that power is no longer conceivable today in our post-Solzhenitsyn era.[3]

The Historian's Pursuit

The Passing of an Illusion is the work of a historian and deals with circumstances, the course of events, modalities. But the ultimate reason for my writing it, if there is one, is beyond me, and I leave the question open. There will always be something mysterious about the nature and scale of the tragedies brought about by the behavior of democratic men and women in the twentieth century. Historians can explain the coming of Hitler by clauses in the Treaty of Versailles and the economic crisis of 1929, but they cannot ignore the fact that these "causes" do not account for the apocalypse wrought by Nazism upon German and European history or, for example, the massacre of the Jews. I am among those who think that when a fact or an event is resistant to historical intelligence, it is better to say so than to pretend the contrary.

I have always had complicated relations with the *Annales*.[1] I don't think the idea of the *événementiel* (the factual) used by Braudel to characterize history—which he disliked, especially political history—is very solid.[2] The fascination of the twentieth century for historians can't be explained by the *événementiel* versus the "structural" but rather by the new, unprecedented character of political regimes like Communism and Nazism. We could say, with Heidegger, that the appearance of those regimes on the stage of history had something to do with the triumph of "technology," so as to express the idea that earlier tyrannies didn't have the same means of constraint at their disposal. But that hardly exhausts the subject.

Something else characterizes totalitarian regimes: the obligation of the tyrannized to proclaim daily their love of the tyrants. George Orwell made this very clear. It wasn't the same under Napoleon: if you weren't conspiring, you didn't have to celebrate the merits of the regime every morning and see it as the preface to a radiant future. I think this obsession with solidarity, with the social bond constantly reaffirmed through the sharing of ideas, is inherent to the dilemma of modern liberalism. In liberal societies there is no common good. Nor is there a collective morality. There are individuals who think what they will about the common good, and who are connected simply by some of their activities. Citizen activity is the least important part of their existence. I can't help seeing the two twentieth-century totalitarianisms not as mandatory products of democracy but as optional products, responses to the formidable question that has trailed through literature ever since Hobbes: if we are autonomous individuals, what constitutes a society? This question crops up all over *The Passing of an Illusion*.

What I wrote was—to use the Kantian expression—a "critical" history: at the beginning of my book I propose a conceptual schema; then I check the facts I have reconstituted and assembled to see whether they give it flesh and substance. I navigate between ideas and facts, going from one to the other and vice versa. I am not a philosopher; I believe historians should avoid doing too much philosophy. If they are mired in the question of the justifications or the limits of their knowledge, they are not writing. There is a middle ground to be found, between positivistic naïveté and nihilistic relativity, an indispensible middle ground today, since we are in a Nietzschean drift: there are no facts, only interpretations. You hear this everywhere: the first student who shows up is full of this short-sighted relativism. It's rather troubling, even though an element of relativism is essential to the construction of an interpretation. But how can you be a historian if you don't unearth facts in order to try to explain them?

In the 1930s, Communist or communistic anti-Fascism was represented in the United States by *Partisan Review,* edited and read by a small group of intellectuals who were either Communists or Trotskyites, New York's equivalent of the Parisian intelligentsia. But they were just a handful of people, a few hundred, mostly Jewish, recent immigrants, many from Central Europe, for whom history was still being played out. For the most part they were superior to French intellectuals and, indeed, were not taken in as long; after all, they were the ones who organized a counter-trial of Trotsky under the presidency of John Dewey.[3] I used to read *Partisan Review* with great interest and saw that it was the same story for the Far Left in New York as in France: there the Soviet trials and the German-Soviet pact alienated the intelligentsia, which in the USSR had rallied to anti-Fascism.[4] A brigade of two thousand Americans fought in the Spanish Civil War in the International Brigades. This is quite impressive. Contrary to what Americans and, especially, the British say today, the Communist idea, although it held little sway over the masses in Britain or the United States, thrived among intellectuals. And on a large scale. Many British intellectuals remained Communists all their lives, impervious to experience.

For the purposes of my book, intellectuals were useful principally as witnesses. I didn't want to write a history of intellectuals. That has already been done.

I don't talk about Sartre, whom I consider an obvious example. I don't need to write ten more pages about Sartre; not because I don't want to talk about him but because so much has already been said, and it's not worth going over it again for the umpteenth time. I much prefer to start afresh—as I do in "Anti-fascist Culture," chapter 8 of *The Passing of an Illusion*—with Bataille, Simone Weil, and Drieu, who are probably more interesting to analyze.[5] But intellectuals are less useful to study as a particular milieu than they are in reconstituting public opinion and ideas in circulation at a particular time. Today, curiously, people think the Communist mystique touched intellectuals for the most part. This is quite untrue. In France, around 1945–46, 25 percent of the vote went to the Communists. If Communism had only touched intellectuals, it could never have achieved, in one century, the dimensions of a collective messianic hope.

The Seductions of Bolshevism

The extraordinary thing about Bolshevism, I wanted to show, was the plasticity of its seduction. Take these three types: Boris Souvarine is the simplest, because he is a Jacobin in the French tradition.[1] Pierre Pascal was a anti-Marxist Christian who adored Russia and the Union des Églises.[2] His case is already harder to understand. As for Georg Lukács,[3] he is even more bizarre: he came from Nietzsche, Kierkegaard, and writers of that kind; he was an aesthete, the son of Jewish banker, an Austro-Hungarian dandy, well known in Budapest's café society and in Vienna. To put it another way, you have three types of intellectuals as different as possible. Then, a little later, the

British Fabians emerged.[4] Bolshevism touched all the intellectual families of Europe. How did the Bolshevik idea managed to gather so many cultural traditions around it—surrealists, Nietzscheans, French Jacobins, British Fabians? The Social Democrats put up a little more resistance, since they were from the same fold and were familiar with Bolsheviks and Bolshevism. But they kept quiet for fear of being called anti-Communists.

The British case is unique, since it involves a Protestant nation and culture. The Bloomsbury group was characterized by an antiestablishment, antibourgeois aestheticism like that of the French surrealists.[5] Pro-Communist by an aestheticizing reaction, this current ran through the English intelligentsia throughout the century; Cambridge in the 1930s is an example. But the Communist Party in Britain, as distinct from that in France, never managed to constitute an electorate and thus a real national presence. Perhaps this is why the British public was not exposed to the theatrical and tragic break-up scenes, of which France offered so many examples: the loyal

militant turned "renegade," denounced in all manner of ways.

✦

The greatest Communist crimes were committed first
against the Russian and then against the Polish — the
forgotten people of Western Europe. Most often, in
Paris, Rome, or London, the historical judgment of
Communism is based on the extermination of the
Russian and Ukrainian peasantry, the millions of
murdered or deported, the Gulag, and Katyn.[6] The
French can be heard making the case for Communism in the name of the Popular Front or paid va-
cations, forgetting that without the split at the Congress of Tours[7] and their ties to the Communists, the
Left would probably have governed France earlier,
and more often.

The Communists' most reprehensible behavior
was in lying about the Soviet regime. We can reproach the Communists much less for what they did
— after all, in a country like France, they were mostly
on the side of the angels — than for what they said, or,

inversely, what they did not say. They never stopped lying. This lie, which today seems so huge, so obvious, was shared and believed to such an extent only because it was not a deliberate deception. In the twentieth century, the lie encountered the passion for democratic universalism of which the Soviet Union was supposed to be the historical legend; that is why it had to be fanatically protected from contamination by forces opposed to violence and dictatorship.

I am struck by the power exerted over our contemporaries by this passion for the universal. Today, in our rich and peaceful countries, the widest avenue to politics for the younger generations is humanitarianism. The rights of man have replaced class struggle, yet serve an identical goal, the emancipation of humanity. I wonder if this isn't just another way of avoiding a really clear look at politics.

Critique of Totalitarianism

My aim was to study the history of totalitarianism, the word and the idea, which emerged in in the early 1920s — in Italy with Mussolinian Fascism, and then in France and Germany — to designate the state's absolute hold over every sphere of social life. But I wrote a chapter on the period of transition between Lenin and Stalin in order to see how the idea of "socialism in one country" caused a shift in the universalistic ambitions of Bolshevism, a shift that brought Bolshevism somewhat closer to Fascism. It was at this point, according to my analysis, that the extension of the totalitarian idea to the Soviet experience appeared in the vocabulary of the time.

The adjective "totalitarian" was born in Italian. As far as I know, it was Mussolini who invented it. In historical semantics, we always tend to push back the birth date of terms; we are never sure we have discovered the first use of a particular word. Still, "totalitarian" seems to have been invented by the Italian Fascists to express the idea of linking all aspects of individuals' lives to the collectivity and the state, as well as the existence of a "total" state that encompasses individuals in all aspects of their lives. Another origin of the word, I think, is the German Right's use of the adjective "total," as in *totaler Krieg*, "total war"; Ernst Jünger used the term "total mobilization."[1] Among members of the German Right, World War I produced the profound idea that the conflict had been a "total war," meaning not so much that the stakes were life and death but that they involved the forces of the warring nations as a whole—not just military virtues among soldiers but all political passions, all capacities of labor. Jünger strongly emphasized the investment of labor in the war, labor as a productive force.

During World War I, the words "total" or "totalitarian" had nothing to do with the Communist universe; in my opinion, it wasn't until the 1930s, when comparable attributes appeared between Nazism and Stalin's Soviet Union, that they took on a dual sense, designating both Fascism and Communism. But we could make a special case for German "National Bolshevism" between 1925 and 1930, a movement that used Stalin's victory and the state that Stalin was in the midst of building in order to provide an example to the German Far Right. I believe the dual sense of "total" and "totalitarian" began at this point. And, as always, the invention of a new word signifies something important.

Defining Communism as essentially anti-Fascism is equivalent to defining it by pure negativity and the traits contrary to those of its adversary: if Fascism was hostile to freedom, then Communism was by definition favorable to it, and so on. This word-for-word contrast, which Marx would have called "idealistic," meaning it existed only on the level of ideologies and intentions, filled the imagination of the European Left. To add some "materialistic" weight to the contrast, the Communists attempted to anchor it in economics, casting Fascism as the product of financial capitalism's final phase: henceforth, the only real anti-Fascist was necessarily anticapitalist and therefore Communist. This thesis is absurd, but the fact that it was so widespread in the twentieth century and so often held for true (which remains the case in certain quarters in spite of the now available historical evidence against it) shows that it draws its strength more from political passion than from intellectual coherence. Once again, we return to Orwell's judgment: the twentieth century Left was anti-Fascist but not antitotalitarian — an excellent summary of the predominant role played by the Communist idea.

The comparison has become taboo because there was a war and there were tens of millions of deaths — Communists who got themselves killed in the name of anti-Fascism. From the end of World War II onward, the intimidating effect of spilled blood was decisive. And no one yet dared to compare Nazism and Communism, because they had faced off on the battlefields and the Red Army had played a powerful and even a leading role in the liberation of Europe from Nazi oppression. No one except for Vassily Grossman,[2] still unknown at the time, and Hannah Arendt, who perceived the analogy very rapidly after the war from the perspective of the camps. But what was taboo just after the war had not been so in the 1930s. At that time, comparing Fascism and Communism under the concept of totalitarianism was quite common. Among my contributions to history is to have shown that the idea of totalitarianism is not at all a post–World War II idea but can be found in the works of many writers during the 1930s.

One such book is Waldemar Gurian's *The Future of Bolshevism*, which is actually about National Socialism: it is extraordinary that a German Jew of Russian origin should have written a book under that title in 1934, a work in which he says that the most perfect form of Bolshevism would be found by the Germans because of their technological mastery. He had already become Catholic. He was the son of

a Saint Petersburg lawyer who had converted to Ca-
tholicism. After his father's death, when Waldemar
was still very young, his mother immigrated to Germany, where he was raised. It was quite complicated:
he was a Russian Jew, a Catholic convert, who wrote
his first books on Maurras and *Action française*.[3] I
discovered *The Future of Bolshevism* by accident, wan-
dering around the stacks of the University of Chicago library—one of the blessings of having books
classified by subject and of the freedom granted to
researchers by American libraries. I remember reading this book with passion, wondering who on earth
this Waldemar Gurian was. I asked some of my col-
leagues, who had no idea, and in the end it was my
friend Reinhart Koselleck[4] who, by telephone, gave
me the keys to this author, who had fallen so rapidly into oblivion in spite of a postwar American ca-
reer. So Gurian imagined, in 1934, that the Bolshevik
project would find its greatest incarnation in Hitler's
Germany.

The same idea emerges in Thomas Mann's *Journal* of that period, replete with Russian-German com-

parisons, Communist Russia appearing as the primitive version of German Nazism. In France, during these same years, the comparison was developed by Simone Weil, in her 1936 writings; by Élie Halévy, in *L'ère des tyrannies* (1937); and by André Gide, after his break with Communism, in his *Journal of 1937–1938*. In 1935, Jacques Bainville published a book under the title *Les dictateurs*, in which he juxtaposed Mussolini, Hitler, and Stalin.[5] In short, the theme was far from rare in the interwar period, whether or not it was associated with the term "totalitarianism." It flourished, of course, between 1939 and 1941, the period of the German-Soviet pact. For *The Passing of an Illusion* I exhumed the American academic colloquium held in 1940 on the theme of totalitarianism, in which the debates centered on both Hitler and Stalin. These debates show that Hannah Arendt, who never cites her sources, wasn't the first to make the fascism/communism comparison but merely reused it in her famous work of 1950, at a time when it had become unmentionable owing to the final course taken by the Second World War. The taboo lasted a great deal longer in Europe, in France and in Italy, for example, than it did in the United States; it has yet to be lifted in Germany. Strangely enough, it made a comeback in American universities in the wake of the Leftist movement of the 1960s.

It's a mystery, which I probably did a better job of describing than explaining, that the political passions of democratic men and women in the twentieth century, a range of emotions, caused them to detest the bourgeois societies in which they lived, to the benefit of extremist ideologies like Fascism or Communism. This hatred of bourgeois society, combining feelings of shame with criticism of its contradictions, is as old as the bourgeoisie itself. It has provided fodder for thought and literature in Germany and France for two centuries. How it brought so many minds, primitive or sophisticated, from such diverse horizons, to embrace the Fascist revolution or the Communist utopia is an enigma I'm seeking to understand. It's a question we try to avoid in our era because, on the one hand, Fascism is seen only in light of its criminality, making it impossible for us to imagine what made it so attractive (and it was indeed attractive), and, on the other hand, we continue to cloak the crimes of the Soviet regime with the excuse of anti-Fascism.

Not only is it a three-way game, but Fascism, liberal democracy, and Bolshevism all share a comparable sense of history. For Fascists, Bolshevism is the future of liberal democracy, because Fascists see liberal democracy as the breeding ground of Bolshevism. For Bolsheviks, to the contrary, liberal democracy is the breeding ground of Fascism, because they believe liberal democracy is bound to become Fascist. Consequently there are three camps, and the one in the middle is merely a passage leading to the two others. In short, for Fascists the truth of liberal democracy is Bolshevism, and for Bolsheviks it is Fascism. Both Fascists and Bolsheviks said as much to anyone who would listen. So both parties could come together against bourgeois democracy, to which both claimed to be the ultimate successors.

The mystery is not that people hate the bourgeoisie. For a democrat, it's "normal" to hate the bourgeoisie; it is a class whose legitimacy comes entirely from wealth, thus a class with no symbolic value, no legitimacy. There will never be a way to make the bourgeoisie into a respectable class, let alone a likable one. Contempt for it is one of the dramas of the modern world. But it doesn't necessarily lead to the horrors that were perpetrated during the twentieth century. The mystery is how badly things went, how criminal the regimes were, and that the antibourgeois passion led to such collective madness. The modern world has been dragging the hatred of the bourgeoisie around with it for three hundred years. And, after all, we live with it. We even make works of art or thought out of it! But how did we go from this lack of legitimacy to the camps, to millions of deaths, to the violence unleashed on bodies and minds? My problem, what I call the "mystery," is the tragic character of the twentieth century.

We must resist the pretension that we have understood or explained everything. It is already an accomplishment to have gotten to the bottom of the political passions of the time, to have reconstituted the complex conditions under which they flourished. But the contrast between the level of civilization of twentieth-century Europe and the savage madness that characterizes its history remains impervious to rational explanation. The collective sadism of the Germans in uniform remains a mystery that Daniel Goldhagen described but did not elucidate.[6]

Hannah Arendt is certainly one of the great witnesses of the twentieth century, though my admiration of her work is not without reservations. Her thinking is often confused, sometimes contradictory, a little demagogic: you can't be simultaneously antimodern, antibourgeois, anti-Communist, anti-Fascist, and anti-Zionist, and in the light of all these rejections still think clearly about the political history of the twentieth century.

There you have it. I think Arendt's historical work is weak—for example, in the first two volumes of *On Totalitarianism* she was not especially concerned with erudition; her knowledge of the Dreyfus Affair

is sketchy, and the same could be said of her gene-
alogy of Fascism. The historical part of that great
book is generally rather weak. What is magnificent
about it is her perception of the tragedy, the camps.
She asserts that this was the first time such a thing
had happened in the history of humanity. And she
was the first to see, along with but independently of
Vassily Grossman—again, they were the only ones,
and both were Jewish, he in the Soviet army and she
in her American exile—that there was something
about those terrible institutions that cannot be explained by Aristotle, Montesquieu, or Max Weber
and that we therefore need new tools to understand
what that something was. What I admire most about
Hannah Arendt is that she sought to describe Fascism and Communism from the standpoint of modern democracy, from the perspective of a society of
individuals, of democratic atomization and technology. As a philosopher, she reinvented the idea of
"totalitarianism." What I've tried to do is to show
that some twentieth-century thinkers had explored

and partially developed this idea before Arendt; she embraced it almost to a fault.

The concept of totalitarianism can always be refuted in the name of those aspects of Nazism and Stalinism that can't be compared, and it can always be defended in the name of those that can. In other words, though I'm not attached to the concept, I can still use it to pinpoint the comparable elements in Stalin's Soviet Union and Hitler's Germany. But when the idea of totalitarianism is pushed to its most rigorous form, and Nazi Germany and Stalin's regime are together seen as forming a new political concept and constituting its empirical substance, that may be going too far.

The passion that made Fascism and Communism what they were was their hatred of a third party. In this connection, Ernst Nolte[7] had an intuition I fundamentally agree with, which is that they should be taken together. There is no other way of thinking historically about these two monstrous products of modern democracy. I don't mean this merely in the

sense that they gave rise to each other through a series of chronological concatenations. I mean it in the
more profound sense that the two democratic visions
of community are, on the one hand, the universality
of humankind and, on the other, the nation. And this
is how it has been since the French Revolution.

I don't think we can understand Nolte without
seeing that in his view there are basically two kinds
of disasters brought about by technology: the Nazi
kind and the Communist kind. The Communist kind
is what Nolte calls "transcendence," that is, people's
passion to go beyond themselves and free themselves
of their finitude, a passion he considers crazy. Nazism, on the contrary, is total immersion in finitude,
a penalty for the impossibility of transcendence. For
Nolte, the two regimes are two forms of the same
problem.

I think Nolte's historical reflection is dominated
by Heidegger, who was his teacher and with whom I
am only superficially familiar. As is clear from the first
chapter of *The Passing of an Illusion*, my philosophic in-

spiration was Tocqueville. My inspiration is Tocque-villian to the extent that I relate the phenomena of Communism and Fascism to the development of "democracy" in the sense Tocqueville used the word. The twentieth century is democracy's first century— the nineteenth was still steeped in aristocracy—and it produced two radical critiques of democracy, one in the form of its universalistic excess, the other in the name of the national or racial community.

This brings me back to the constitutional ambi-guity of the idea of a world of equality, which can lead to freedom but also to unprecedented forms of despotism. These latter forms, revealed, alas, by the twentieth century, offer tragic illustrations of hu-man freedom. In moral or even theological terms, the exercise of liberty was driven spectacularly, in the twentieth century, by the problem of evil. This is the mysterious part of our history, the part that would culminate in Auschwitz. I don't share Ernst Nolte's philosophical presuppositions. But he re-mains a great historian and is, indeed, more of a historian than a philosopher. He was the first, in his 1963 book *Der Fachismus in seiner Epoche*,[8] to set out the great landscape of ideas, today forgotten or censored, that formed the background of Fascism and contained elements common to the Far Left. At that time, in my opinion, he was already too quick to link Communism with Fascism, either through their Mussolinian connection or through the reactive relationship of Fascism to Bolshevism. But he uses a trove of knowledge of the entire European scene following World War I, and he shows what was new about it. I have trouble understanding the smear campaign against him in Germany. Nolte is certainly a conservative, suffering from Germany's fate in the twentieth century, but he is an anti-Nazi conservative, even radically anti-Nazi, for he believes that Hitler destroyed German tradition and culture. With regard to the Jews, he is in no way tempted by Holocaust denial, as has sometimes been insinuated; he is, to the contrary, perfectly clear on this issue.

We could perhaps reproach Nolte for his exoneration of the German people. The idea that there was no *particular* responsibility on the part of the Germans, that the massacre of the Jews could have been committed by others and, moreover, was preceded by Soviet crimes, reveals a preoccupation that seems understandable. In his book on Fascism, mentioned earlier, the first volume is about Maurras. I couldn't help thinking it was no accident he chose a French political thinker as the precursor of Fascism, when in fact, Maurras's positivism is hardly comparable to the irrationality that characterizes Fascist thought.

In one of the recent conversations I had with Nolte, I returned to an idea that in my view is false: that Nazism and Fascism were simply consequences of Bolshevism. For Nolte, the basic element of Nazism is anti-Marxism, anti-Communism, and he makes the chronological sequence into a causal one: Hitler was a product of Lenin. And of Stalin. This leads him to erase endogenous sources, the German sources of Nazism. He seeks to separate Nazism from its German roots. But at least he raises the question of the history of Nazism, which today has been re-

pressed by substituting abstract moralism for an understanding of the past.

Renzo De Felice was a positivist historian;[9] unlike
Nolte, he hated philosophy and maintained that facts
spoke for themselves. He was somewhat naïve epis-
temologically and didn't appreciate the huge amount
of preliminary work required by all historical writing. His biography was similar to mine: he was a
Communist until 1956. Sadly, he died recently—I
am writing his obituary for the Italian press. I think
there was a moment, as is always the case when
someone leaves the Communist Party, when he took
off his ideological glasses: he saw things differently,
truthfully; he opened his eyes. De Felice was critical
of Communist anti-Fascism before I was, correctly
seeing it as a self-seeking way of masking what separates Communism from democracy. He also wrote a
work on Italian Fascism, a probing study of the political and intellectual roots of the movement which,

in Italy, was more to the Left than to the Right: the tradition of the *Risorgimento,* of the socialist Far Left. The part of De Felice's work that caused the greatest stir was the third volume of his biography of Mussolini, in which he explains that Mussolini was one of the most popular personalities in Italian history, and in European history generally, between 1929 and 1936.

The very definition of totalitarianism is problematic, and I tend to think that Fascist Italy fits only partially into this framework, since the monarchy and the Catholic Church remained powerful and were, for the most part, appeased and respected by Mussolini. The regime was not anti-Semitic until 1938. It became so only by analogy with Hitler. There were even a number of Jews in the Fascist party in the 1920s and 1930s.

In Italian history, Fascism was not an apocalypse: the regime ended in 1943, when the Fascist Grand

Council removed Mussolini, and that was something highly unusual. What the Italians never say, and what De Felice shows so well, is that many former Italian Fascists, who had become Communists between 1943 and 1945, turned up in the Resistance, hostile to the Salò's Republic. This is an open secret in Italy: many members of the postwar Italian Communist Party came from Fascism. Moreover, and De Felice explains this in his books, many of the characteristics of postwar Italian democracy are inherited from Fascism — the role of the trade unions, mass parties, the industrial sectors of the state.

De Felice was an extraordinary historian, a bit narrow-minded philosophically but possessed of amazing erudition. His biography of Mussolini will long remain the authoritative one; simply, prosaically, like a positivist historian, he presents a chronological history of Italian Fascism. And he does so with a great deal of impartiality, which of course earned him twenty years of misunderstanding and insults. In the end, as it the case with all good books, his was the one that carried the day.

✦

I well remember the return of the French Jews from deportation. It's a very strong memory. I was eighteen. The revelation of the camps made a huge impression on me. The French Jews didn't return from the camps as Jewish martyrs but as French ones. (There is a good book on this subject, incidentally, by Annette Wieworka).[10] Being assimilated French Jews, they felt, quite naturally, that it was as French citizens that they had been persecuted. But a more important point is that Communists during this period wanted to be considered the major victims of Nazism. They sought to monopolize the place of the victim: they mounted a formidable operation of victimization after the war. I'm not suggesting that this was pure invention, that they had not actually been persecuted by Fascism. That would be absurd. What I mean is that they exploited their anti-Fascist struggle all the more massively because it had been periodically eclipsed, as was the case between 1939 and 1941. In Eastern Europe, Jewish martyrdom was systematically concealed so as not to dwarf the militant Communists' role, or that of the "Soviet" people, as the anti-Fascists of choice. This is pretty hard to imagine now that the situation has reversed, and our contemporaries, when considering the crimes of Nazism, are tending to focus exclusively on the massacre of the Jews.

Hitler was incontestably brought to power by a segment of the German ruling classes, the right-wing political circles, but he only assumed power because he was there. In order to be in the right position, he had to have convinced a large part of the masses. In other words, he wasn't put into power by the German ruling circles like a puppet. In fact, he had been knocking at the gates of power for a long time. He had a rank and file, money, and so forth. And he took this opportunity to liquidate all of his opponents. This was so much the case in 1934 and 1935 that all open political dissent in Germany had become impossible. I call this the Nazi revolution, or the beginning of totalitarianism. The attraction Hitler exercised over the masses predated his assumption of power and was independent of the political elites. His revolution, however, occurred in 1933 and 1934, after he had seized power thanks to the blindness of the German parliamentary Right, which he would smash as he did the Left. The revolution was the reduction of the entire society to submission and silence, broken only by obligatory proclamations of loyalty to the Nazi regime. This is the characteristic that brings Hitler's Germany closest to Stalin's Russia: the tyranny of an ideological party-state, a tyranny so complete that the subjugated are under constraints even in their private lives, even within their families.

The most important feature of such a regime is the state's total control over social life, the reduction of civil society to a complete absence of autonomy. So I think Italy is a special case, because Fascist Italy never reached the degree of political enslavement experienced by Nazi Germany. That said, in Russia and Germany we find a party of the masses; the omnipresence of ideology; a slightly different role for the head of state in the Fascist and Communist systems, more important in Nazism than in Communism: the functional aspect of the head of state in the Communist regime is more accentuated than it was in the Nazi regime. So the two regimes resembled each other as far as daily life was concerned, and both were quite new when compared to traditional forms of despotism. What strikes me favorably about the word "totalitarianism," as long as it is used with precision, is that these regimes were new. There was no preexisting word for them. Just as the word "individualism" appeared between 1820 and 1830 in France because the thing existed and had to be named, so the word "totalitarianism" had to be invented because the thing existed, and the word was invented precisely to characterize Nazism and Stalinism. I don't see how we can do without this word. I believe those who don't accept the concept do so for reasons that are less than respectable, partisan reasons. I don't know what term they could substitute.

"Tyranny" is a term typical of the classical antiquity. It doesn't take into account the democratic side of the totalitarian phenomenon. The democratic side is what produces the ideological aspect, for in order to create solidarity among the masses, a body of common beliefs is needed, promulgated by the party or the head of the party and characteristic of this new kind of monarchy: a totalitarian monarchy. Totalitarianism is a product of democracy and the masses' entry into history, a theory we find in Hannah Arendt but rarely in other, less important thinkers; Western political science seems impermeable to the Tocquevillian idea of democracy—the idea that the equality of individuals opens the way not only to liberty but to despotism. And there is always a tendency to associate political liberty with the word "democracy."

What is magnificent about Tocqueville is his conviction that a new era for humanity had begun at the moment when people, meeting together, considered themselves as equals. Equality of conditions does not mean that people are equals, but it does signify anthropologically that a modern human being, when encountering a fellow human being, believes him- or herself to be equal to that person. And Tocqueville understood that this was a revolution in the history of humanity.

Learning from the Past

We should probably increase our tolerance of conflicts and tensions. For the worst thing we can do is to imagine that we will someday do away with humanity's division. What surprises me is how intolerable we find that division, how we modern citizens are constantly searching for unity among ourselves, trying to find a solution through politics since there is no longer any religion. And we can't find a solution. We must accept living in an amputated, damaged state, living in finitude and division. Nonetheless, I think it's essential to reflect on the lessons of the twentieth century. The psychological investment in salvation by history has revealed itself to be a catastrophe.

My concern about how little we reflect on what happened is one of the reasons I wrote *The Passing of an Illusion*. Soon, no one will even know what Communism was. Ten years ago, Communism was still familiar; it existed; people had a vague notion of what it had been, the world it represented.

I think modern citizens have a moral and spiritual equilibrium that comes primarily from their relation to the past. And in seeking to create individuals cut off from tradition and their history, we're on our way toward a world peopled with individuals who are prisoners of technology, superstitions, lifestyles, and so on. Consequently, the historical experience of modern democracy, which isn't very old, only two or three hundred years, is the basic groundwork today, at the end of the twentieth century, for learning to live together. Without it, we will never come up with a democratic politics. Earlier, I mentioned rights: we live in a world where human rights have become our civil religion. Talk to young people today, it's the only idea they have. It's not much of an idea, and is of no help in formulating any thoughts about the world situation or our near future. Reflecting on the past is the only pedagogy useful for throwing light on our political behavior. Otherwise we are condemned to angelism, seeing the world as if everyone were perfect, which would lead at best to impotence, at worst to fanaticism.

But we can make a distinction between the historian's profession, which consists of looking at the past with a concern for the truth, and political pedagogy, which would turn it into a message for citizens. In no way am I saying that this political pedagogy should be transparent, but it must nonetheless address the great notions of living together. Today, under the pretext that Fascism dishonored the nation, we no longer have a clear conception of nation. This is particularly visible in Germany, where the nationalist excesses led to the disaster of which we are so well aware. Young Germans today can say quite casually that the construction of Europe consists of uniting certain provinces—for example, Wurtemberg with

Languedoc, Bavaria with Brittany: this is obviously a mask, concealing the problems that divide Germany and France. For the peoples of the world, the nation remains the principal form of living together, even though a broader configuration is emerging in Europe, beginning with the economy. But we are becoming less and less capable making space for national questions. Take the drama in Bosnia, born typically of national conflicts, although treated by the press and intellectuals in the West as a tragedy of humanitarian universalism.

It is the illusion of universalism that keeps us from thinking about such conflicts in terms of national bodies. We live in a time when we would like to go beyond the phenomenon of nation, but politics still revolve largely around national passions. That is why history, as it has for the last two hundred years in democratic nations, still has a very important role to play, the role of a pedagogical moral authority.

We hardly know what the military is anymore, although it clearly remains an indispensible dimension of political and collective life. We will continue to have local wars. We won't have any more world wars, but we will have a series of local conflicts over passions that have become foreign to us. They will have to be arbitrated. Even the ending of obligatory military service in France, a good thing in itself, has a melancholy aspect: the army was one of the last places where different generations and classes got to know one another. Its dismantling amounts to a re-inforcement of private individualism. This is a major trend in our late twentieth-century societies, quite natural given the decline of political thinking, dishonored jointly by Fascism and Communism.

We proclaim equality while forming societies obsessed by the conquest of nature, by the passion for ownership, and by that most universal of distinctions, money, which was instrumental in the dissolution of hierarchies and thus an instrument of equality before becoming the measure of inequality. In the United States, money is both "democratic" and inegalitarian. In France, Bernard Tapie made his mark in a period when money played an egalitarian role, which enabled him to do well, to rise;[1] he is still perceived, although very rich and of questionable ethics, as a man of the people. Giscard d'Estaing,[2] on the other hand, who comes from inherited money, is just a rich bourgeois. It is in the United States that the historically democratic function of money is most evident: there, the social status of individuals depends less on family or ancestral position than, quite bluntly, on money earned. So there is more mobility in fortune and rank, a general acceptance of the arbitrage of money; For Americans, there's no honor in poverty. The ideal democratic society would be a society where the privileges of birth and thus the right to inherit are abolished. But what citizen would accept this attack on natural sentiments? Here we return to the "limits" of democracy.

Tocqueville is probably the author who understood most profoundly that democracy tends toward the integration and homogenization of individuals by way of a passion for equality. This process of integration and homogenization is never finished, and even as it advances, it deepens feelings of frustration. We need only look at today's society, preoccupied with the discourse of "exclusion," while history has never seemed more "inclusive." Social exclusion was much more widespread in the nineteenth century, to say nothing of the preceding centuries, but far fewer people spoke of it or made it the center of political discourse. The exclusion of the workers, which was only too massive and too real, was treated in terms of class struggle. Today, the discourse of exclusion is abstract, universal, and omnipresent, as is the related, somewhat ritualistic idea of human rights.

Introduction

1. In an interview published in the *Nouvel Observateur* in November 1978, François Furet, undoubtedly in error, stated that he joined the French Communist Party in 1947.

2. François Furet, "1789–1917: aller et retour," *Le Débat*, no. 57 (November–December 1989): 4–15.

3. Jean-Louis Panné, "Esquisse d'une critique de la critique du *Passé d'une illusion*," in *François Furet: Révolution française, Grand Guerre, communisme*, edited by Pierre Statius and Christophe Maillard (Paris: Cerf, 2011), 46–47.

4. *Le Cercle de minuit*, 26 November 1996, talk show hosted by Laure Adler on France 2, Inathèque (library of the Institut National Audiovisuel).

5. François Furet, *Le passé d'une illusion: Essai sur l'idée communiste au XXe siècle* (Paris: Robert Laffont / Calmann-Lévy,1995); translated by Deborah Furet as *The Passing of an Illusion: The Idea of Communism in the Twentieth Century* (Chicago: University of Chicago Press, 1999).

6. Pierre Rigoulot, "La réception du *Passé d'une illusion*," in Statius and Maillard, *François Furet*, 27.

7. *Le Débat*, no. 89 (March–April 1996), including contributions by Renzo De Felice, Eric J. Hobsbawm, Ernst Nolte, Richard Pipes, and Giuliano Procacci.

8. *Le Cercle de minuit*, 1 February 1995 and 25 April 1995, hosted by Laure Adler on France 2, Inathèque.

9. Denis Berger and Henri Maler, *Une certaine idée du communisme: Répliques à François Furet* (Paris: Éditions du Félin, 1996), 7.

10. See, for example, Perry Anderson, "Dégringolade" and "Union sucrée," *London Review of Books*, September 2 and 23, 2004; François Cusset, *La décennie: Le grand cauchemar des années 1980* (Paris: La Découverte, 2006); and Michael Christofferson, *Les intellectuels contre la gauche: L'idéologie antitotalitaire en France,1968–1981* (Marseille: Agone, 2009). Enzo Traverso, in "Marx, l'histoire et les historiens: Une relation à réinventer," *Actuel Marx*, no. 50 (October 2011): 154, strangely considers François Furet to be part of a "Conservative school," alongside his great enemy Richard Cobb.

11. Furet, *The Passing of an Illusion*, 518.

12. Ernst Nolte, "Une histoire brève qui finit tristement," in Statius and Maillard, eds., *François Furet*, 14–16. See François Furet and Ernst Nolte, *Fascisme et communisme*, Nolte's letters translated by Marc de Launay (1998; Paris: Hachette littératures, 2000).

13. Nolte, "Une histoire brève," 21.

14. Fonds Paul Ricoeur, library of the Institut protestant de théologie, Conf. 168, Boîte 51. Unpublished letter from François Furet to Paul Ricoeur 22 September 1996. I would like to thank Catherine Goldenstein and Olivier Abel for their effective and kind guidance in the Paul Ricoeur archives. François Dosse, in his biography *Paul Ricoeur: Les sens d'une vie, 1913–2005* (Paris: La Découverte, 2008), never once refers to François Furet. Many thanks as well to Élisabeth Dutartre, archivist of Francois Furet's archives at the École des hautes études en sciences sociales, for her valuable help.

15. *Bulletin de la Société française de philosophie*, 1989, 83rd year, 3rd meeting, 156.

16. Ibid., 167.

17. François Furet and Denis Richet, *La Révolution française*, 2 vols. (Paris: Hachette, 1965–1966).

18. In Furet's copy of Ricoeur's *Lectures I: Autour de la politique* (Paris: Seuil, 1991), the author had written on the title page: "For François Furet, an exploration, through the thinkers we hold in esteem, of the public space in which you dwell as a great historian. Paul Ricoeur."

19. Paul Ricoeur, *La critique et la conviction: Entretiens avec François Azouvi et Marc de Launay* (Paris: Calmann-Lévy, 1995).

20. Archives of the Fonds Paul Ricoeur, Institut protestant, Conf. 168, Boîte 51.

21. François Furet to Paul Ricoeur, 22 September 1996, ibid.

22. François Furet to Paul Ricoeur, 6 March 1997. This letter exists in both archives, that of the Fonds Paul Ricoeur, Institut protestant, Conf. 168, Boîte 51, and in the François Furet archives, CESPRA-EHESS.

23. François Furet et Paul Ricoeur, 22 September 1996.

24. François Furet to Paul Ricoeur, 6 March 1997.

25. Ibid.

26. Ibid.

27. Ibid.

28. Arte (French public TV arts channel), 2005, Inathèque.

29. First transcription, Archives François Furet, CESPRA-EHESS.

30. Second version, ibid.; and below, "On the Nation."

Ideas and Emotions

1. See François Furet, *Marx et la Révolution française, suivi de Textes de Karl Marx, réunis, présentés et traduits par Lucien Calvié* (Paris: Flammarion, 1986). Translated by Deborah Furet as *Marx and the French Revolution* (Chicago: University of Chicago Press, 1988).

2. Ferdinand Lasalle (1825–1864) was the founder, in 1875, of the German Socialist Party. Jules Guesde (1845–1922) was the founder of the first French Marxist Socialist Party. Jean Jaurès (1859–1914), a moderate, was a founder of the French Socialist Party. Louis Blanc (1811–1882), a French republican and socialist, was the author of a twelve-volume history of the French Revolution. Pierre-Joseph Proudhon, a French journalist and socialist, is regarded as the father of anarchism.

On the Nation

1. Joseph de Maistre (1753–1821), a politician, historian, and philosopher, fostered political thinking hostile to the French Revolution.

2. See, for example, Zeev Sternhell, *La droite révolutionnaire, 1885–1914: Les origines françaises du fascisme* (Paris: Seuil, 1978).

The Socialist Movement, the Nation, and the War

1. Benjamin Constant (1767-1830) was a liberal Franco-Swiss politician. Auguste Comte (1789-1857), French philosopher and sociologist, was founder of the philosophical school of positivism.

2. Arno Mayer, *The Persistence of the Old Regime: Europe to the Great War* (New York : Pantheon Books, 1981).

The Past and the Future of the Revolution

1. See François Furet, *Penser la Révolution française* (Paris: Gallimard, 1978). Translated by Elborg Forster as *Interpreting the French Revolution* (Cambridge: Cambridge University Press, 1981).

2. Georges Lefebvre (1874-1959), a man of the Left, was inspired by Karl Marx and Marc Bloch. He was the author of *Le Grand Peur de 1789* (Paris: Armand Colin, 1932). Translated by Joan White as *The Great Fear* (New York: Pantheon Books, 1973).

3. Alexander Solzhenitsyn (1918-2008) was the author of the *Gulag Archipelago* (1973).

The Historian's Pursuit

1. The *Annales* was a historical journal founded in 1929 by Marc Bloch and Lucien Febvre. They were associated with the Sixth Section of the École pratique des hautes études, which in 1975 would become the École des hautes études en sciences sociales and of which François Furet was president 1977-85.

2. Fernand Braudel (1902-85), a historian of economics and of Mediterranean societies, was a major figure in the *Annales* school.

3. John Dewey (1859-1952), a psychologist, philosopher, and educational theorist at the University of Chicago, organized the Dewey Commission in Mexico City, which in 1938 cleared Trotsky of accusations made against him by Stalin.

4. In Moscow, on 23 August 1939, the German foreign minister Ribbentrop

and the Soviet prime minister Molotov signed a nonaggression pact between the USSR and the Third Reich.

5. Georges Bataille (1897–1962) was a member of the Cercle communiste démocratique founded by the former Communist Boris Souvarine in the interwar period. Simone Weil (1909–43) was a philosopher engaged in the trade union movement and a member of the Cercle communiste critique. Drieu La Rochelle (1893–1945) was a writer drawn both to Stalinist Communism and to Fascism, for which he opted in the end.

The Seductions of Bolshevism

1. Boris Souvarine (1895–1984) was the name assumed by Boris Lifshitz. After being a leader of the French Communist Party, he was expelled in 1924 for criticizing the "Bolshevization" of the party. He published a biography of Stalin in 1925.

2. Pierre Pascal (1890–1983) was an academic and a militant Catholic. Impassioned by Russia and the Russian language, he was sent to Petrograd in 1916 by the French military. In 1917, he went into the service of the Russian Revolution; he returned to France in 1933. The Union des Églises was a movement that sought to unify the Russian Orthodox and Roman Catholic churches.

3. Georg Lukács (1885–1971) became a Marxist in 1917 and joined the Hungarian Communist Party. Exiled in Austria, in Germany, and then in Moscow, he returned to Budapest in 1945. He was banished again after the insurrection of 1956 but returned a year later.

4. The Fabian Society was a British left-wing group created in 1884. Its members included George Bernard Shaw, H. G. Wells, and Beatrice and Sidney Webb.

5. The Bloomsbury group, created in London in the early nineteenth century, included such writers as Virginia Woolf, E. M. Forster, Lytton Strachey, and Roger Fry.

6. In Katyn, a forest near Smolensk, the Soviet political police murdered several thousand Polish officers and other key figures in the spring of 1940.

7. When the French Socialist Party held its Congress at Tours in 1920, the majority voted to join the Third International and create a new organization; the minority split off and maintained the Socialist Party.

Critique of Totalitarianism

1. Ernst Jünger (1895–1998), a veteran of World War I, left an extraordinary testimony of the war in his book *In Stahlgewittern* (Berlin: E. S. Mittler und Sohn, 1920). Translated by by Michael Hofmann as *Storm of Steel* (London: Penguin Classic, 2004).

2. Vassily Grossman (1905–64), a Russian Jew who joined the Red Army, was among the first to write about the Nazi extermination camps, which he discovered by entering Treblinka. After the war, he distanced himself from the Soviet regime, which confiscated his great book *Life and Fate*, in which he painted a portrait of Soviet society during the war. (The book would be published in Switzerland in 1980.)

3. Charles Maurras (1868–1952), prolific journalist and writer, a leader of the right-wing movement *Action française*, he was imprisoned after World II for having supported the Pétain government.

4. Reinhart Koselleck (1926–2006), a German historian, was a founder of the history of concepts and the epistemology of history.

5. Jacques Bainville (1879–1936) was a journalist, historian, and visceral anti-Communist. His book appeared in English translation, *Dictators*, in 1937.

6. See Daniel Jonah Goldhagen, *Hitler's Willing Executioners* (New York: Alfred Knopf, 1996).

7. Ernst Nolte, born 1923, is a German historian and author of *Der europaïsche Bürgerkrieg 1917–1945: Nationalsozialismus und Bolshevismus* (Munich: Herbig Verlagsbuchhandlung, 1975). After the publication of *The Passing of an Illusion*, in which François Furet wrote a long note about Nolte, the two historians engaged in a long correspondence. See François Furet and Ernst Nolte, *Fascism and Communism*, translated by Katherine Golsan, preface by Tzvetan Todorov (Lincoln: University of Nebraska Press, 2001).

8. Nolte's book was translated by Leila Vennewitz as *The Three Faces of Fascism* (New York: Henry Holt, 1966).

9. Renzo De Felice (1929–96) was a member of the Italian Communist Party but left it after the repression of the Budapest uprising. His monumental biography of Mussolini was published in 1995.

10. Annette Wieworka, *L'ére du témoin* (Paris: Plon, 1998).

Learning from the Past

1. Bernard Tapie, born in 1943, is a businessman who became Minister of the City in the Socialist government of Pierre Bérégovoy in April 1992.

2. Valéry Giscard d'Estaing, born 1926, was elected president of France in 1974.